ANIMALS AND THEIR YOUNG

Field and Garden Babies

ANIMALS AND THEIR YOUNG

Field and Garden Babies

Penny Stanley-Baker
Illustrated by Vladimir Savitsch

Collins

BLACKBIRD   Not just a sweet song, a sweet tooth too . . .

Father blackbird really is black all over, save for his bright yellow bill and the yellow ring around his eye. Mother blackbird is just like him in shape and size, but brown. Blackbirds sing so sweetly that nobody really minds them helping themselves to the strawberries and raspberries in the garden.

In Spring when the time comes to build their nest, the blackbirds are soon too busy for song. Often they return to the nest they built the year before, which may be in need of repair. Blackbirds are not shy and may build their nest close to your house. Father blackbird helps gather the twigs, grass and mud needed for the nest, but he leaves the building to mother blackbird, who knows just how it should be done.

Soon she is sitting on four or five blue-green eggs.
About two weeks later the baby birds are clamouring
to be fed, and father and mother take it in turns to
go in search of fat juicy earthworms, insects, spiders
and centipedes to pop into their wide-open beaks.

Baby blackbirds start fluttering around long before they can fly. For the last few days before they take off on their own, their parents are still busy feeding them in between flying lessons. Half of them tag along behind their mother, while the others follow their father, badgering him for food. Once they have all flown, the parents will soon be rearing another brood.

WOODMOUSE   A few tell-tale nutshells and a tiny hole

Woodmice don't go out much in the day. They prefer to go foraging at dusk or dawn when they can't be seen. With their big eyes and ears and keen sense of smell, they can find their way even on the darkest night.

If it senses danger, a woodmouse will tuck up its front paws and go bounding away on its hind legs like a kangaroo, or vanish up a tree.

In Spring and Summer woodmice eat seeds, fresh buds and shoots, worms and snails. When Autumn comes they begin to collect nuts and pine cones for the Winter ahead. These they store away under a log, in a crack in the wall or even in an empty bird's nest. Before doing so, they carefully nibble a little hole in the corner of each nut and strip the cones of their scales.

Mother woodmouse makes her nest underground, at the foot of a tree or in an old mole burrow. Some grass, a few leaves and some moss make a soft warm

lining for the nest. The five or six baby mice have no fur to keep them warm and are blind at birth. By the time they are ten days old their fur has grown and their eyes open. Within three weeks they are ready to go scampering off in search of their own food and their own homes.

WOODPECKER Carpenter-in-chief

That loud hammering in the tree over there is the woodpecker, busy drilling a hole with its long straight bill. Into the hole goes its sticky pointed tongue, to scoop out the insect beneath the bark.

The woodpecker moves up the tree in a series of little hops, head cocked, listening. It grips the trunk with its four strong claws, while its stiff tail feathers act as a prop.

Woodpeckers make their nest inside the tree trunk. They pick a tree where the wood is soft or rotten, but hollowing out the nest is hard work. First they must make an entrance, then they carefully carve out a tunnel leading to the rounded nesting chamber. This they line with wood chippings.

The mother sits on the eggs throughout the day. Father woodpecker takes over at night. When the chicks hatch they have no feathers at all, but no harm can come to them deep inside the tree with

mother woodpecker to keep them warm. A tap on a special part of the bill tells the chicks it's feeding time, and their bills open wide for a tasty caterpillar or grub. As they grow, the young woodpeckers make their way to the light and crowd round the entrance, waiting to be fed. Soon their sharp little bills are hacking away at the bark in search of insects to eat.

RABBIT   If you want to lie low, go underground!

Long ears pricked, nose a-twitch, the rabbit sits up on its haunches listening. Scenting danger, it sounds the alarm with a firm thump of its hind foot, before scuttling to safety, its bobbing white tail a warning to other rabbits to do likewise.

Rabbits like being with other rabbits. They make their homes underground by burrowing down where the earth is soft. This underground network of burrows and tunnels is called a rabbit warren.

Baby rabbits are born in special burrows called 'stops'. A stop has only one entrance. Mother rabbit lines the far end with soft grass and moss. Two days before the babies are born, she plucks some fur from her tummy to make the nest really snug.

Baby rabbits are born blind and deaf, without any fur. But inside the stop they are so warm and safe that mother rabbit can leave them there all day,

returning only at dead of night to feed them. Each time she leaves her babies, she carefully blocks up the entrance with earth.

In two weeks the baby rabbits' fur has grown and they begin to explore. Within a month they are eating grass like fully-grown rabbits and perhaps even raiding the farmer's crops or the neighbour's vegetable patch.

ROOK Safety in numbers

Being part of a big noisy family has its advantages.
There's always someone to give the alarm or to fly on
ahead to check that the coast is clear. Rooks live
together in large numbers – the more the merrier.
Sometimes hundreds, even thousands of rooks will
make their home or 'rookery' in a clump of tall trees.

In the Spring mother and father rook start collecting twigs, grass and roots. These mother rook binds together with mud to make a deep cup-shaped nest. Rooks often return to the same nest year after year and patch it up. Mother rook lines the nest carefully with blades of grass, even strands of sheep's wool. Once she's satisfied, she settled down to lay the first of her four or five eggs. In the rook family, mother does the sitting.

It is two weeks before the eggs hatch and mother rook sits on the baby birds a full ten days after that. While father rook works hard to feed his wife and young, mother rook keeps the nest spotlessly clean by removing the baby rooks' droppings in her beak.

The young rooks are soon strutting around clumsily on the edge of the nest. They leave the nest when they are three or four weeks old. Some may venture further afield, but most of them will be happy to stay with their brothers and sisters in the rookery where they grew up.

MOLE   A loner in a labyrinth

It's easy enough to see where a mole has been, but you won't often see the mole itself. Molehills are the mounds of fresh earth the mole throws up when it tunnels underground. Moles are made for tunnelling. They have strong front paws to dig with, and a velvety coat which does not collect earth. They find their way more with their ears and noses than with their eyes. They can even run backwards underground holding their little tails upright to guide them.

The mole's run is also its larder. Into the run drop the earthworms and insects the mole feeds on. In Winter, moles tunnel deeper down where the earth is warmer and make fresh runs.

When Spring comes, father mole goes in search of a wife. After a few hours mother mole shoos him away. Three weeks later her babies are born underground in a hollow nest of straw and dry leaves the size of a football. The nesting chamber has more than one entrance by which mother mole can come and go in search of food. In the first weeks the baby moles feed entirely on their mother's milk. Later she teaches them how to hold an earthworm between their front paws and bite off its head to stop it burrowing back into the earth again.

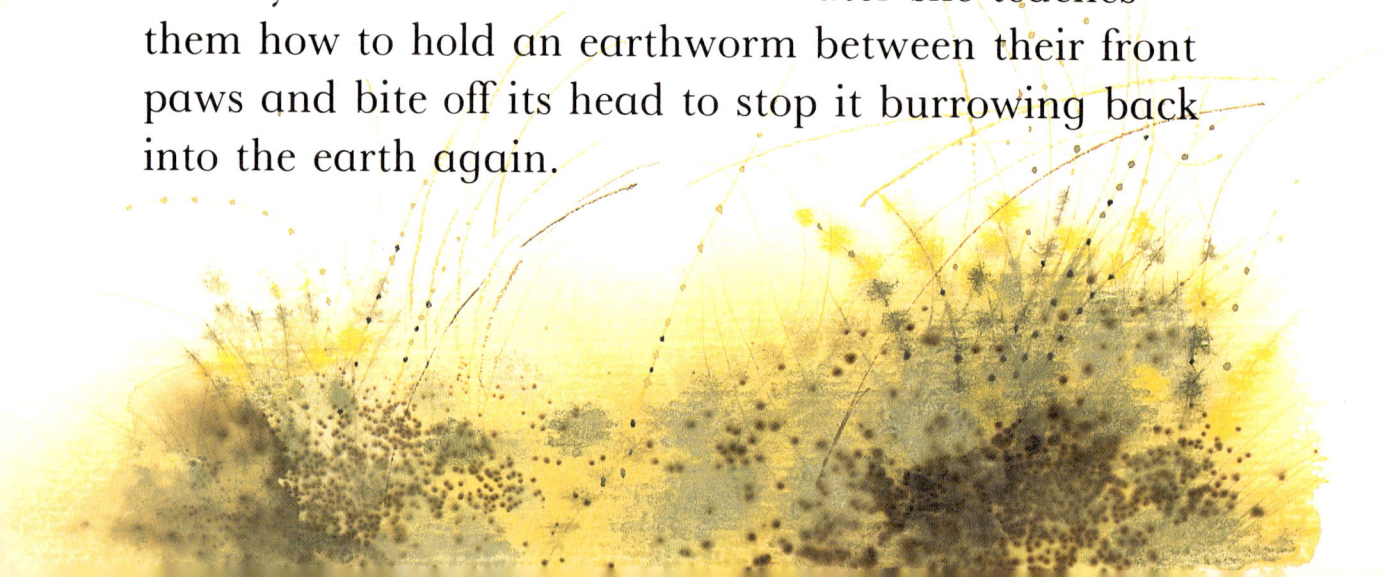

Sooner or later the baby moles find their way out into the open. On these outings they learn to beware of hungry owls or passing herons.

Once the babies are old enough to fend for themselves mother mole sends them on their way with a sharp nip on the backside and returns alone to her burrow for another year.

COLLARED DOVE   Two's company . . .

A pair of collared doves coo contentedly from the branches of a tall pine tree. Each has a narrow black collar fringed with white running round the back of its neck. These doves often gather in large numbers to feed, but once they have eaten, they return to their separate nesting places.

The nest the parent birds build has to last longer than most because collared doves lay eggs even in Autumn and Winter. They will need a roof over their heads in the cold so the parents usually choose an evergreen tree that will not lose its leaves in Winter. Collared doves are not the neatest of nest-builders.

Their nest is just a flimsy little platform of twigs so loosely put together that from underneath you can sometimes see the eggs through the gaps. Mother dove lays two eggs only. Father and mother take it in turns to sit on them.

Baby doves are called squabs. Squabs are fed in a special way. The parents don't bring them worms or insects to eat. Instead they open their beaks wide and let the squabs drink a sort of rich milk from inside their throat, called crop milk. When the squabs are bigger, their parents feed them seeds and grain. Soon the rickety nest can hold them no longer, and the young doves fly off to make their homes elsewhere.

First published in the UK in 1988 by William Collins Sons & Co Ltd,
8 Grafton Street, London W1X 3LA.

ISBN 0 00 190004–8